Character Education
Resource Guide

Written by
Regina G. Burch

Editor: Teri L. Fisch
Illustrator: Jane Yamada
Cover Illustrator: Kathi Ember
Designer: Corina Chien
Cover Designer: Corina Chien
Art Director: Tom Cochrane
Project Director: Carolea Williams

This book is dedicated to my parents, James and Ruth Griffin, whose daily lessons in character guided my life.
Thank you to my husband, Michael, and our sons, Kitt and Brian, for providing the inspiration and understanding that have made my writing possible.

Table of Contents

Introduction

Do you struggle with teaching children to persevere, be responsible, and exhibit honesty?

Teach children positive values and stress the importance of practicing them by incorporating the program presented in the *Character Education Resource Guide*. Use the activities and stories in this resource guide to teach children about what types of actions define a person of good character. Teach them that *character* is an individual's pattern of behavior but also includes a person's thinking and feeling as well. Explain that it means choosing to do the "right thing" on an everyday basis. It is important that you model good behavior and stress the importance of children being good citizens in all situations for them to internalize these lessons. This comprehensive character education program will help you teach children how to make themselves, the school, and their community friendlier and happier.

Make teaching good character traits meaningful to children by incorporating the traits and activities in this resource into your classroom. The *Character Education Resource Guide* identifies 12 character traits and provides definitions for these traits, related literature, and hands-on activities to introduce children to the traits. It also features reproducible mini-books to link character education with beginning reading.

This program will help you begin to build a community of children who practice positive character traits and recognize the impact of these traits in their own lives as well as the lives of others. The activities are the perfect complement to your classroom curriculum and can easily be incorporated into your current teaching program. They enable you to integrate children's learning about character traits with their academic subjects. Use the 12 reproducible mini-books (one for each character trait) to integrate character education into your reading curriculum. Double your instructional time by using these mini-books to teach children important character-building values while they practice prereading, reading, and postreading skills and strategies.

As you incorporate this character education program into your daily teaching, you will be amazed at the differences you begin to notice. Watch as the children in your classroom build their way toward a more caring classroom community!

Getting Started

Use the information and activities provided in this resource to highlight a different character trait each month. Introduce each character trait to the class by defining it and discussing what actions exhibit the trait. Have children participate in character-building activities included in this resource, and have them read the corresponding mini-book to help them understand the trait. Give children incentives to practice good character traits (see page 7), and invite them to share their learning with their family (see Family Involvement on page 8). Extend children's learning by inviting them to create role-play scenarios about each trait. This activity will help them reflect on their actions and the consequences of their actions.

Connecting with Literature

Introduce each character trait to your class by reading aloud books from the following literature list or others with similar themes. Discuss the character trait, and ask children to reflect on whether or not the characters in the story displayed the trait.

Acceptance
Freckle Juice by Judy Blume (Yearling Books)
Marsupial Sue by John Lithgow (Simon & Schuster)
The Sneetches and Other Stories by Dr. Seuss (Random House)

Compassion and Caring
Mrs. Katz and Tush by Patricia Polacco (Bantam Books)
Pierre by Maurice Sendak (HarperCollins)
Wilfrid Gordon McDonald Partridge by Mem Fox (Kane/Miller)

Cooperation
The Five Chinese Brothers by Claire Huchet Bishop and Kurt Wiese (Econo-Clad Books)
Seven Blind Mice by Ed Young (Philomel)
Swimmy by Leo Lionni (Alfred A. Knopf Books)

Courage
Amazing Grace by Mary Hoffman (Dial Books)
A Bad Case of the Stripes by David Shannon (Scholastic)

Friendship
Frog and Toad series by Arnold Lobel (HarperCollins)
The Rainbow Fish by Marcus Pfister (North-South Books)

Generosity
A Chair for My Mother by Vera B. Williams (Greenwillow Books)
The Giving Tree by Shel Silverstein (HarperCollins)
Johnny Appleseed by Steven Kellogg (William Morrow & Company)

Good Judgement
Hey, Little Ant by Phillip and Hannah Hoose (Tricycle Press)
Strega Nona by Tomie dePaola (Simon & Schuster)
Which Would You Rather Be? by William Steig (HarperCollins)

Honesty
The Berenstain Bears and the Truth by Stan and Jan Berenstain (Random House)
A Big Fat Enormous Lie by Marjorie Weinman Sharmat (Dutton)
The Empty Pot by Demi (Henry Holt and Company)

Perseverance
John Henry: An American Legend by Ezra Jack Keats (Alfred A. Knopf Books)
Three Cheers for Tacky by Helen Lester (Houghton Mifflin)
Whistle for Willie by Ezra Jack Keats (Penguin Putnam)

Respect
Big Al by Andrew Clements (Aladdin)
The Lorax by Dr. Seuss (Random House)
William's Doll by Charlotte Zolotow (HarperCollins)

Responsibility
A Day's Work by Eve Bunting (Houghton Mifflin)
Miss Rumphius by Barbara Cooney (Viking)

Self-Discipline and Self-Control
David Goes to School by David Shannon (Scholastic)
Ronald Morgan Goes to Bat by Patricia Reilly Giff (Penguin Putnam)

Character Education Mini-Books

Each of the 12 sections contains one mini-book reproducible of a Creative Teaching Press Character Education Reader. Each 16-page mini-book focuses on teaching children about one character trait. Choose a trait, copy a class set of the corresponding mini-book, and put one together for each child using the following directions.

Putting Together the Mini-Books

Make double-sided copies of the corresponding mini-book. (Make sure the book is facing the same direction on the copier when you copy the front and back.) Place the pages in a pile in the order they appear in this guide. Trim the edges of the copies. Then, fold the pages in half lengthwise (on the dotted cut line). Cut the pages on the cut line, fold the pages on the solid fold line (so the title page is on the front), and staple them together to make one 16-page book.

Or, make double-sided copies, trim the edges of the copies, and cut the pages in half lengthwise on the dotted cut line to make four strips. Use the dots in the center of the strips to stack book pages in sequential order, with the four-dotted strip on the bottom of the stack and the one-dotted strip on top. Fold the strips in half (so the dots are on the inside of the book), and staple them together to make one 16-page book.

Using the Mini-Books

Divide the class into small guided reading groups. Invite children to use prereading strategies to discuss the title and character trait of the book prior to reading. Introduce key vocabulary and difficult words children will encounter. While children read, ask questions and review the text to increase their comprehension. After children read, invite them to discuss the character trait.

Successful vs. Unsuccessful

Materials
- ❤ assembled mini-books (see page 5)
- ❤ chart paper

Ask each guided reading group to discuss how the characters in their mini-book were successful and unsuccessful in portraying the character trait. Draw a 2-column chart on a piece of chart paper. Title the columns *Successful* and *Unsuccessful*. Record, or invite children to record, all of the characters' actions that exhibited the trait and all of the actions that did not. For example, for the mini-book *Telling the Truth*, children can write *Emily answers questions truthfully* under the heading "Successful" and *A girl tried to cheat on her test* under the heading "Unsuccessful." Encourage children to reread the story and look at the pictures to help them find examples for each column. Ask children to evaluate whether the characters in the story practiced good character traits.

Book Box

Materials
- ❤ cereal boxes (1 for each child)
- ❤ scissors
- ❤ mini-books

Have each child make a "book box" out of a cereal box and store all the mini-books in it. Have children cut off the front panel of the box and place their books in their box. Invite children to decorate their box. Have them store their book box in the classroom or take it home to reread stories for independent reading.

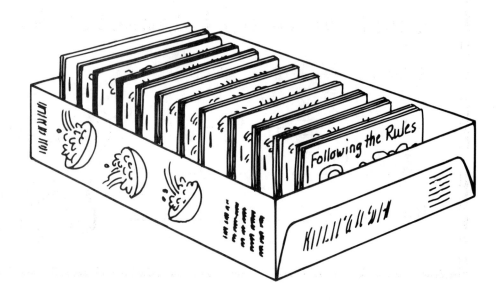

Reward Certificates

Directions: Copy the certificates on colored paper, and cut them apart. Decorate a shoe box with stars. Cut a small hole in the top of the shoe box. Write the name of the character trait children are learning about on a piece of paper, and attach it to the box. Every time you "catch" a child displaying the character trait, give him or her a certificate to place in the box. At the end of each day, choose a certificate from the box, and give the chosen child a small reward (e.g., pencil, eraser, sticker). At the end of the month, host a special lunch for all the children who received a certificate or for the children who received the most certificates.

CAUGHT BEING GOOD!

_____

displayed the character trait of

_____ today!

_____
Date

BUILDING GOOD CHARACTER AWARD

This certificate is given to

_____

on _____

for being _____!

Family Involvement

In order for children to internalize and practice the character education traits you are teaching them at school, these traits must be emphasized in the home as well. At the beginning of the school year, tell parents about the character education program you are incorporating into your classroom. Invite them to carry their children's learning into the home. Encourage parents to read the reproducible mini-books with children when they bring home the books and to talk to them about the trait in each story.

Each month, send home a letter to inform parents of the trait your class will be focusing on. Explain what types of activities the children will be completing at school and what types of behaviors you will be looking for in your classroom. Encourage parents to read the letter to their child and discuss the trait with him or her. Ask parents to "pounce" on teachable moments by pointing out to their child that they did a good job exhibiting a positive character trait. For example, a parent might say *Thank you for being responsible and cleaning up your toys after you played with them.* Suggest ways parents can reinforce their child's learning at home:

- ♥ Read a story with your child and talk about what good and bad character traits the characters in the story possess.
- ♥ Look in newspapers or magazines with your child and find articles about people who performed deeds that showed good character.
- ♥ Talk to your child about historical figures and the character traits and contributions they made to the country and the world.

Stress to parents the importance of being good role models themselves as they make decisions and are faced with difficult situations. Invite parents to

- ♥ help their children make good decisions as situations come up.
- ♥ role-play situations with their children to help them understand the consequences of their actions and to help them see what decision they should make in the future when faced with a similar situation.
- ♥ talk to you about the character traits and to share ideas with you about additional activities your class may enjoy.

Tap into the resources available to you through the children's families and the community to help you develop children's understanding of what good citizens do and how they act.

Acceptance

understanding and appreciating unique qualities in others

Melting Pot Cookbook

Discuss diversity and the value in understanding and appreciating various cultures. Give each child a My Family's Recipe reproducible. Ask children to interview family members to learn more about their cultural heritage. Tell them to write at the top of the reproducible the name of one country in which their ancestors lived. Then, have children write a family recipe from that country. (Help children find a recipe in an ethnic cookbook if their family does not know one.) On a designated day, have children bring in foods made from their recipes for a "diversity luncheon." Have each child introduce the food by telling its name and country of origin. After the luncheon, collect the recipes. Make a class set of copies, and bind together the pages to make a Melting Pot Cookbook for each child.

Materials
- ♥ My Family's Recipe reproducible (page 10)
- ♥ ethnic cookbooks
- ♥ foods (prepared by children)
- ♥ bookbinding materials

A Unique Quilt

Tell children that each of them has similarities and differences. Explain that it is important to accept people's differences because that is what makes every person unique and special. Give each child a construction paper square. Have children create a "quilt square" by drawing a diamond in the center of their paper. Have children work in pairs to interview each other. Tell children to ask each other questions to help them discover four unique qualities about the person and write each quality in a corner of their quilt square. (You may choose to have the class brainstorm questions to ask prior to the interview.) Have children glue a photo of their partner in the diamond and write the person's name above or below the photo. Invite children to decorate their quilt square. Laminate the squares, hole-punch the sides, and connect them with yarn to make a "quilt." Display it in the classroom, and invite children to read the quilt squares to learn about the many unique qualities of their classmates.

Materials
- ♥ white construction paper squares
- ♥ crayons or markers
- ♥ glue
- ♥ photo of each child
- ♥ yarn

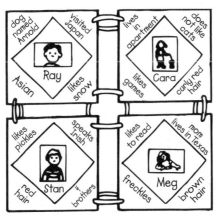

My Family's Recipe

by _____

My ancestors lived in the country of _____.

This is a recipe for _____.

Ingredients

Recipe Directions

Character Education Resource Guide © 2003 Creative Teaching Press

Everyone is special and unique, you will find.
So accept people's differences and always be kind.

So accept people's differences and always be kind.

Fold Here

Everyone is special and unique, you will find.

Dancers of the World

Everyone Is Special and Unique

Learning about Acceptance

Character Education

Regina G. Burch © 2003

Show understanding for one another.

10

Inside we're all alike, you will see!

15

But you should like your friends for who they are.

7

Your friends may look very different from you,

2

POPCORN 3

MAIN ENTRANCE

Fold Here

Character Education Resource Guide © 2003 Creative Teaching Press

Treat others with kindness and get along with each other!

14

When problems happen, we should talk till we agree.

Your friends may sing well or be a football star,

9

But they have the same feelings that you do.

3

Fold Here

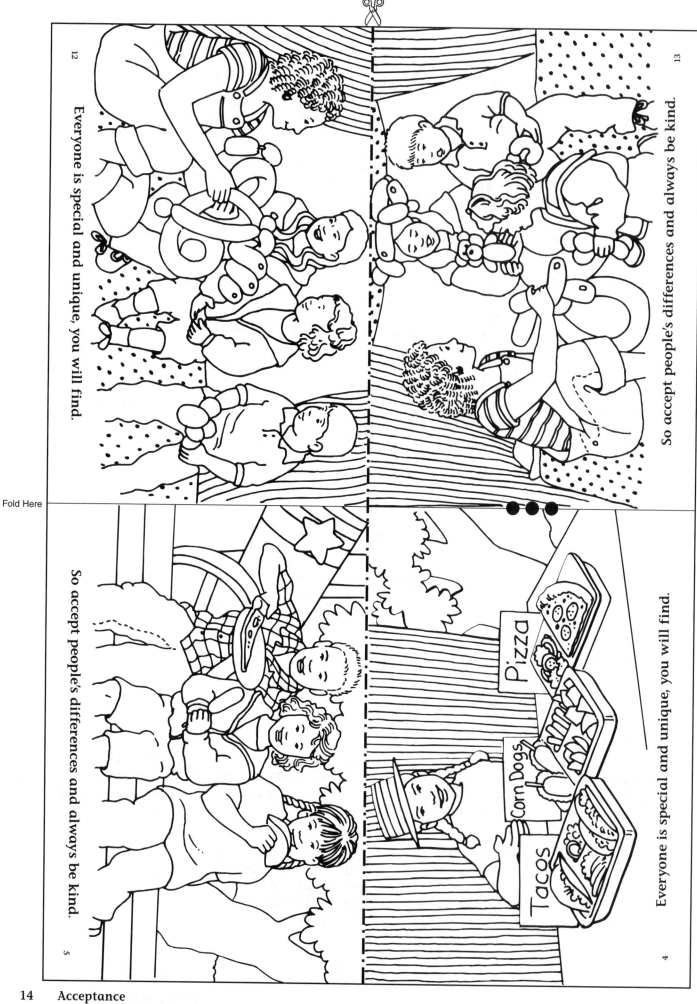

Everyone is special and unique, you will find.

So accept people's differences and always be kind.

So accept people's differences and always be kind.

Everyone is special and unique, you will find.

Pizza

Corn Dogs

Tacos

12

13

5

4

Fold Here

Compassion and Caring

empathizing with others and acting on those feelings with care and concern

Caring Brings Sunshine

Discuss with the class the need for compassion and caring for people who are sick. Plan a visit to a hospital or nursing home. Ask the administrator to pair each child with an adult who enjoys the company of children. During the visit, invite children to spend time reading stories and talking with their partner. Take a photograph of each pair. After the trip, develop the photos. Give each child a Sun's Rays reproducible, and have children glue their photograph on the center of the sun. Then, have them cut out the sun and its rays. Ask children to write on the rays things they did with their partner that showed compassion and caring (e.g., *I hugged Marty, I looked at pictures of Marty's grandson*). Invite children to glue their sun and its rays on a piece of construction paper. Give these pictures to the children's partners with wishes for good health.

Materials
- ❤ Sun's Rays reproducible (page 16)
- ❤ camera/film
- ❤ glue
- ❤ scissors
- ❤ construction paper

Illustration: A sun with a photo of a child and adult in its center, labeled "Sydney and Joy." The rays read: "We played checkers.", "I made her laugh.", "I got Joy water.", "I read a story.", "We looked at pictures.", "I told jokes."

The ABCs of Compassion

Ask children to share ways they show compassion for others. Assign each child a letter of the alphabet. Have children identify a way to show compassion that begins with their assigned letter and write a sentence using their word (e.g., I can <u>help</u> my brother with his homework, I can <u>compliment</u> my friends on their clothes). Have them highlight their word by underlining it or writing it in large bold letters. Invite children to draw an illustration above or below their sentence. Bind together children's pages into a class alphabet book of compassion. Read the book to the class, and share each child's illustration. Have children say something they like about each page and compliment its creator. Place the book in the classroom library for rereading.

Materials
- ❤ drawing paper
- ❤ crayons or markers
- ❤ bookbinding materials

Sun's Rays

Character Education Resource Guide © 2003 Creative Teaching Press

Friends may have a change of plans.

Star Reader

Compassion is understanding someone else's needs. So show that you care with your good deeds.

Fold Here

Give a helping hand.

Show You Understand
Learning about Compassion and Caring

Character Education

Regina G. Burch © 2003

Show you understand.

10

Listen to him read.

15

Someone may have dropped their books.

7

Someone may be new at school.

2

Character Education Resource Guide © 2003 Creative Teaching Press

Fold Here

11

Compassion is understanding someone else's needs.
So show that you care with your good deeds.

14

Brother may need help with homework.

Fold Here

9

Compassion is understanding someone else's needs.
So show that you care with your good deeds.

3

Give a welcome smile.

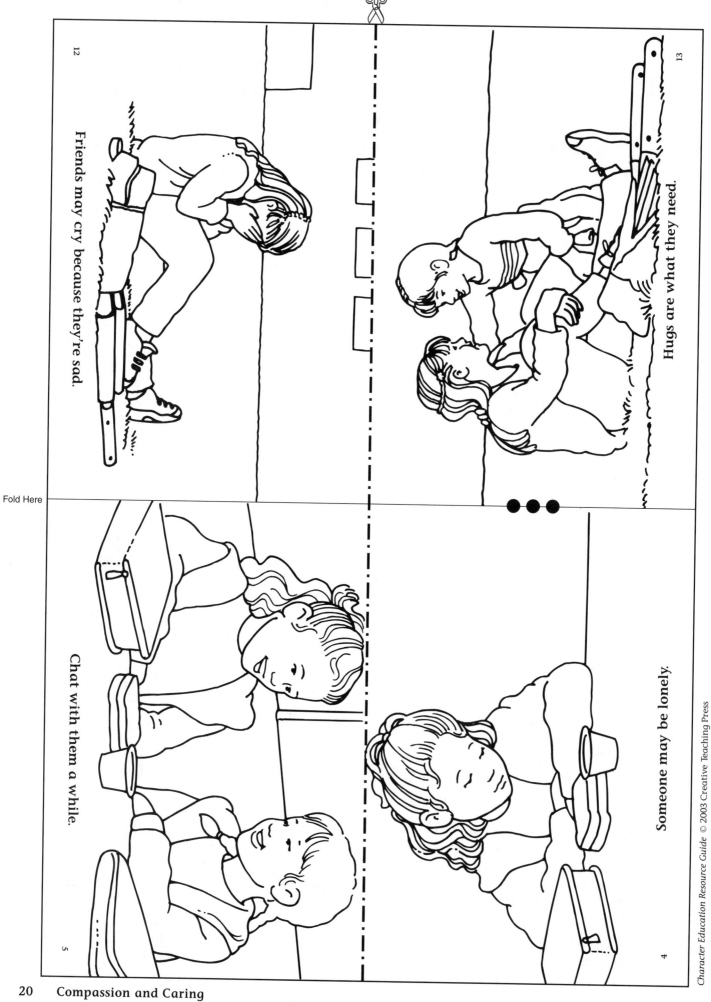

12

Friends may cry because they're sad.

13

Hugs are what they need.

Chat with them a while.

5

Someone may be lonely.

4

Character Education Resource Guide © 2003 Creative Teaching Press

Cooperation

willingly working with others toward a common goal

Seven Blind Mice

Copy a class set of the Elephant reproducible on gray construction paper. Read aloud *Seven Blind Mice*. Discuss how, individually, each mouse had difficulty determining the identity of the mystery object. Explain that when the mice worked together as a team and shared their ideas, they discovered the object was an elephant. Have volunteers name classroom tasks that would be easier if completed as a group (e.g., cleaning up the classroom at the end of the day). Chart suggestions on the chalkboard. Divide the class into groups of five. Give each group an Elephant reproducible. Invite each group to choose a classroom task and write it on their paper below the elephant. Ask children to lightly color a different body part of the elephant (e.g., trunk, tail, ear) and write a way they can help complete that task on their body part. Display the elephants on a bulletin board surrounded by mouse cutouts.

Materials
- *Seven Blind Mice* by Ed Young
- Elephant reproducible (page 22)
- gray construction paper
- colored pencils or crayons
- mouse cutouts

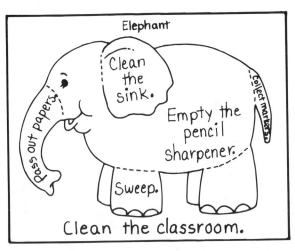

String Game

Cut a piece of yarn for every three children. Divide the class into groups of three. Tell children they will work together silently to manipulate their yarn to form objects on the ground. Name several easy- and hard-to-make objects (e.g., triangle, star, house, your state or country). After several rounds, have children discuss the cooperation necessary to play the game. Relate the cooperation needed in the game to that in the classroom. As an extension, play this game when studying specific subjects such as geometry (shapes), science (animal homes), or grammar (punctuation marks).

Materials
- 5' (1.5 m) yarn pieces

Elephant

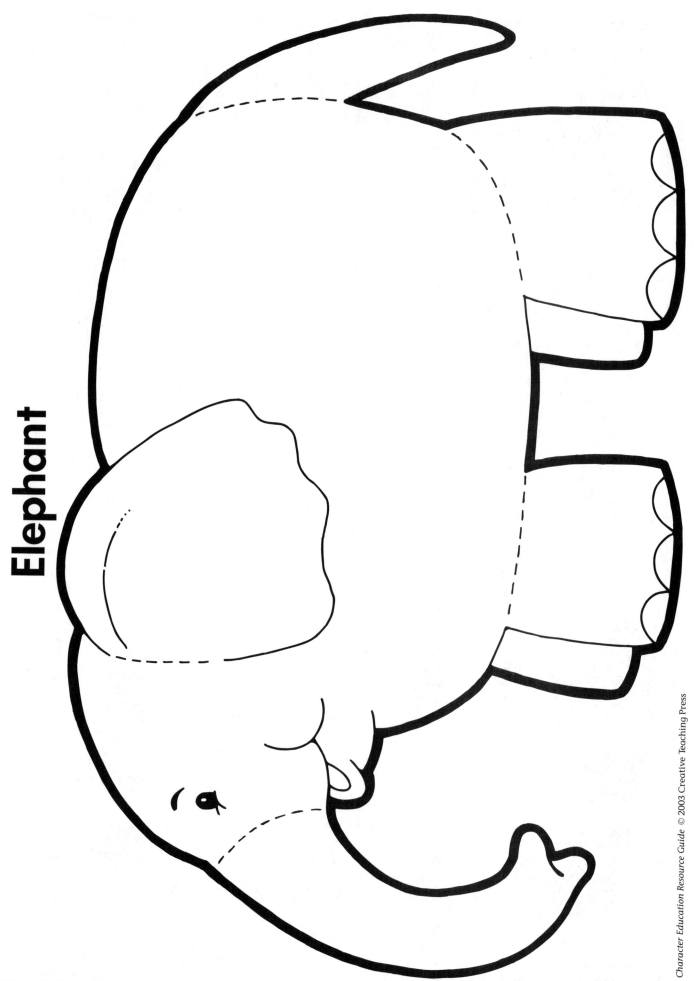

Character Education Resource Guide © 2003 Creative Teaching Press

Carrot
Juice
10¢

Why should I do what others expect of me?

Fold Here

Cooperate to reach your goals in work and play.

Character Education

Working Together

Learning about Cooperation and Citizenship

Regina G. Burch © 2003

8

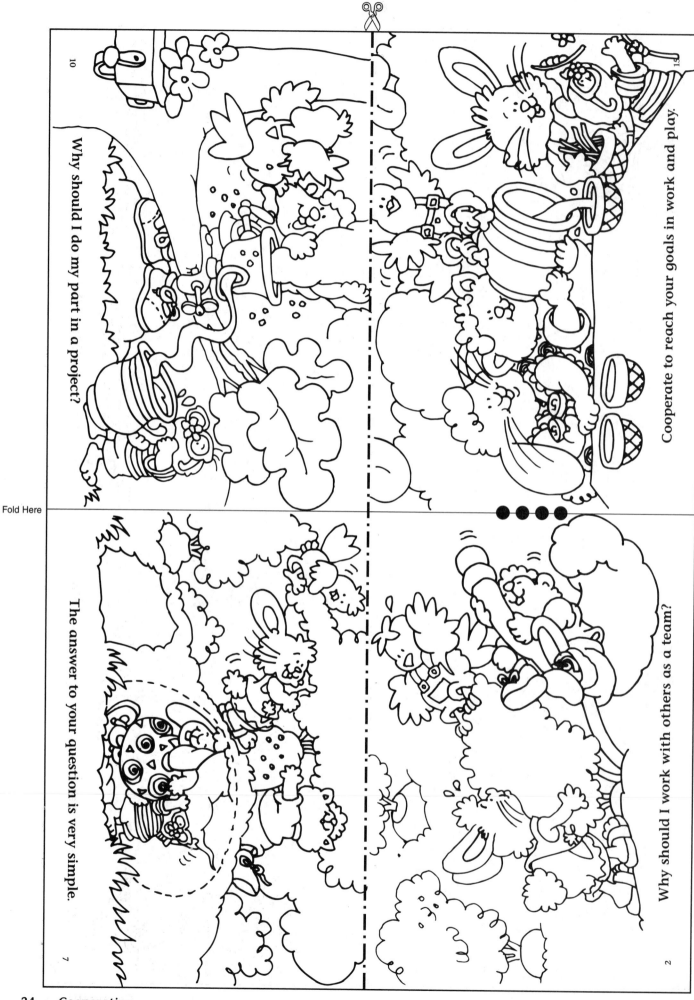

10

Why should I do my part in a project?

Cooperate to reach your goals in work and play.

Fold Here

The answer to your question is very simple.

7

Why should I work with others as a team?

2

The answer to your question is very simple.

Carrot Juice 10¢

Why should I take the time to meet with others?

Carrot Juice

Fold Here

• •

Why should we discuss everyone's ideas?

Cooperation's the way to work together each day.

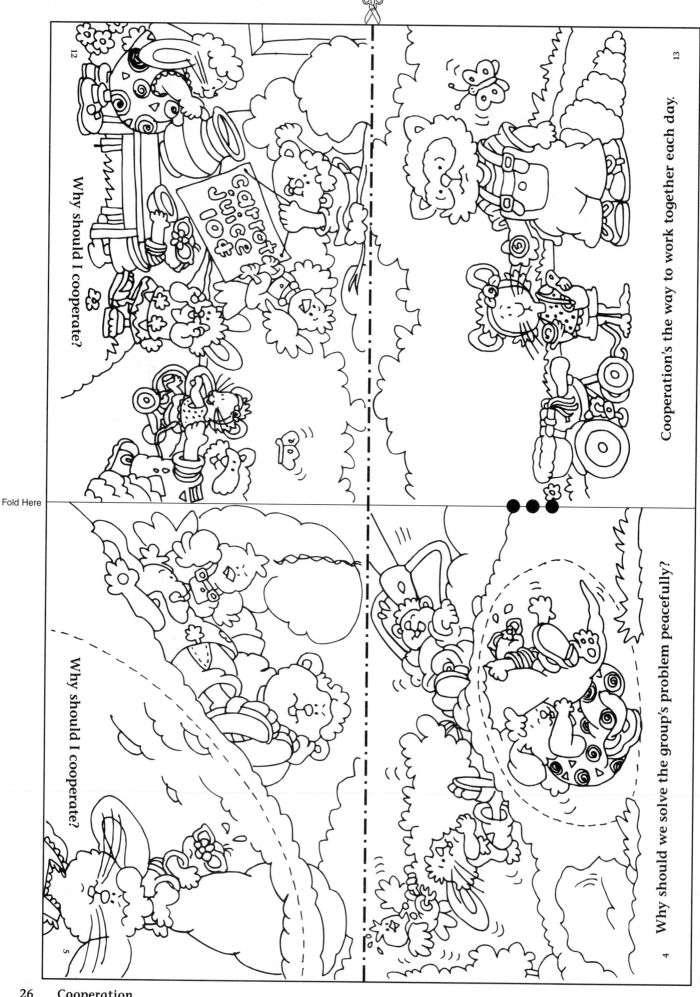

Why should I cooperate?

12

Cooperation's the way to work together each day.

13

Why should I cooperate?

5

Why should we solve the group's problem peacefully?

4

Character Education Resource Guide © 2003 Creative Teaching Press

Courage

standing strong for your own beliefs and doing what's right even when others disagree

Sequence the Story

Give each child a David's Bike Helmet reproducible and a construction paper strip. Ask children to cut apart the story cards. Then, have them put the cards in the correct order to show the story of how David performed a courageous act (wearing his bike helmet and standing up for what he knows is right even though another child made fun of him for it). When children correctly sequence the story cards, invite them to color the pictures. Then, have them glue the cards in the correct order on their paper strip. Discuss the story cards with the class. Ask children to explain what is happening in each picture. Have children explain how David was courageous. To extend the activity, invite children to write the story shown on the cards.

Materials
- ❤ David's Bike Helmet reproducible (page 28)
- ❤ 4" x 24" (10 cm x 61 cm) construction paper strips
- ❤ scissors
- ❤ crayons or markers
- ❤ glue

Not Fighting Is Courageous

Discuss with the class why it takes courage to walk away from a fight. Invite a police officer or community leader to visit your classroom to discuss this, the consequences of fighting, and why it is important to settle matters in a nonviolent manner. Ask the class to also discuss how it is important to stand up for what they believe in even though it may not be a popular idea with others. Record children's ideas on chart paper. Invite children to illustrate and write about what they should do and why they should not fight with others (e.g., you should walk away from an argument to avoid confrontation, if you get in a fight you could say mean things and hurt someone's feelings). Display children's work, or bind the pages together to make a class book. To extend the activity, take the class to the school library to find books about leaders in history who had the courage to stand up for unpopular beliefs (e.g., Abraham Lincoln, Martin Luther King, Jr., George Washington, Mahatma Ghandi). Encourage children to read about these leaders and share the information with classmates.

Materials
- ❤ chart paper
- ❤ drawing paper
- ❤ bookbinding materials (optional)

David's Bike Helmet

Directions: Cut apart the story cards. Put the cards in the correct order to show the story of how David performed a courageous act. Color the pictures. Glue the cards on a construction paper strip in the correct order.

Go after your goals, and make yourself proud.

and make yourself proud.

Fold Here

Character Education

Dare to Have Courage

Learning about Standing Strong

Go after your goals,

8

Regina G. Burch © 2003

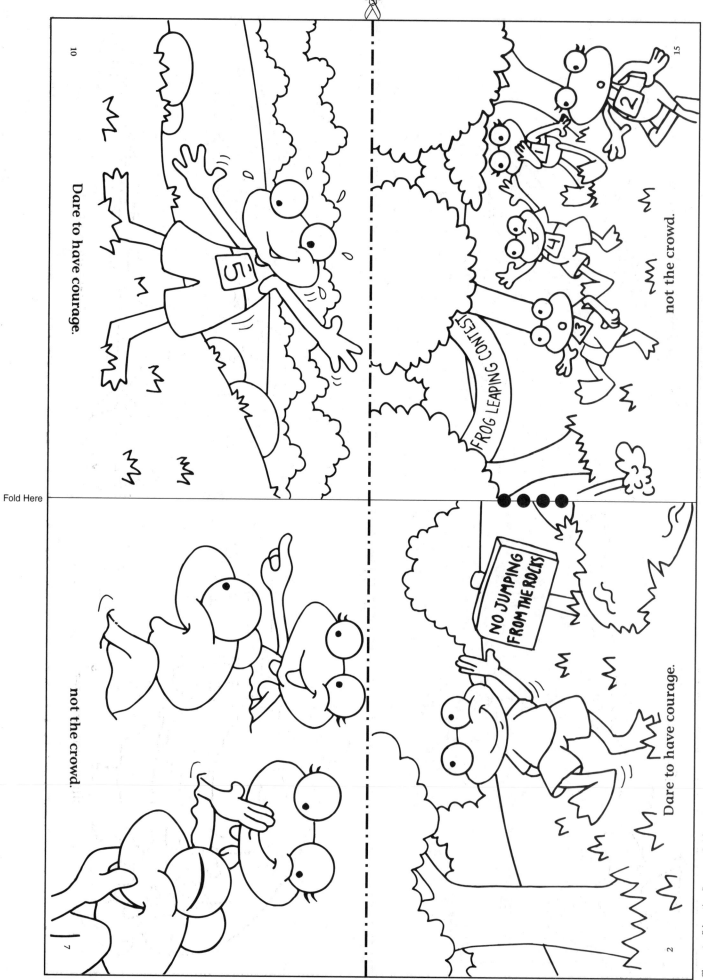

Follow your conscience

Do what's right.

Do what's right.

Follow your conscience

WORLD RECORD

Fold Here

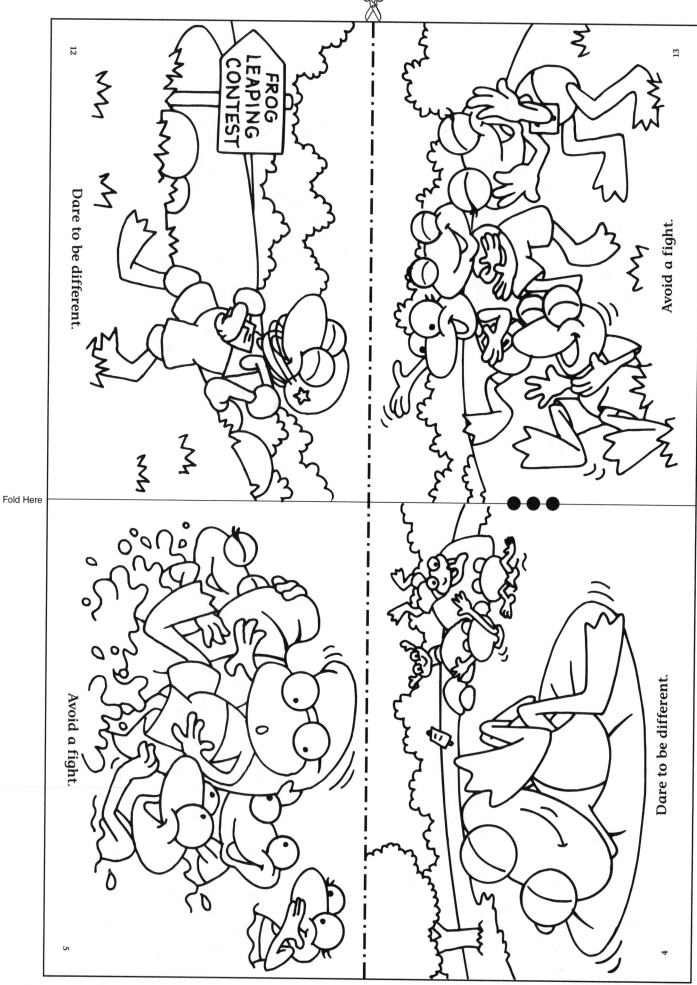

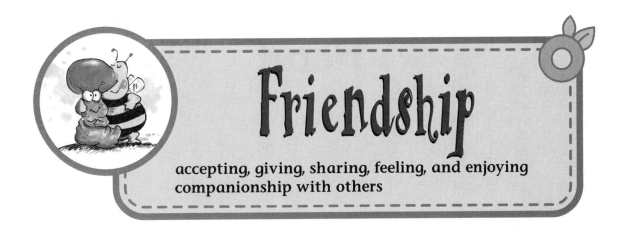

Friendship

accepting, giving, sharing, feeling, and enjoying companionship with others

Caring Hearts

Discuss friendship with the class. Discuss different ways to show friends you care about them. Record children's responses on chart paper. In advance, make several copies of the Heart reproducible on tagboard, and cut them out to make patterns for children to trace. Have each child use a pattern to trace a heart on construction paper. Have children refer to the chart paper and write a sentence that explains how they show a friend they care about him or her. Invite children to illustrate their sentence and cut out their heart. Hole-punch children's hearts and a Heart reproducible (to use as a book cover). Use a heart-shaped key ring or a metal ring to bind together the pages to make a class book about friendship. Read aloud the book to the class, and encourage children to read it independently.

Materials
- ♥ Heart reproducible (page 34)
- ♥ tagboard
- ♥ scissors
- ♥ chart paper
- ♥ construction paper
- ♥ crayons or markers
- ♥ hole punch
- ♥ heart-shaped key ring or metal ring

Wanted: A Good Friend

In advance, copy "want ads" from a newspaper on overhead transparencies. Invite the class to brainstorm characteristics and qualities that make a good friend. Write the list on chart paper. Display the transparencies. Discuss with the class what information is included in a want ad, and tell children they will create a want ad for a new friend. Have children draw on construction paper a picture of their requirements for a friend or write a descriptive paragraph. Display the completed ads on a bulletin board titled *Wanted: A Good Friend.*

Materials
- ♥ "want ads" newspaper section
- ♥ overhead projector/ transparencies
- ♥ chart paper
- ♥ crayons or markers
- ♥ construction paper

PHAN
Wanted: Best friend. Funny, honest, must like model airplanes. Bike rider a plus. See Phan for more information.

Sophie
Wanted: Best Friend
happy
shares books
roller blades

Heart

Good Friends
Love
Each Other!

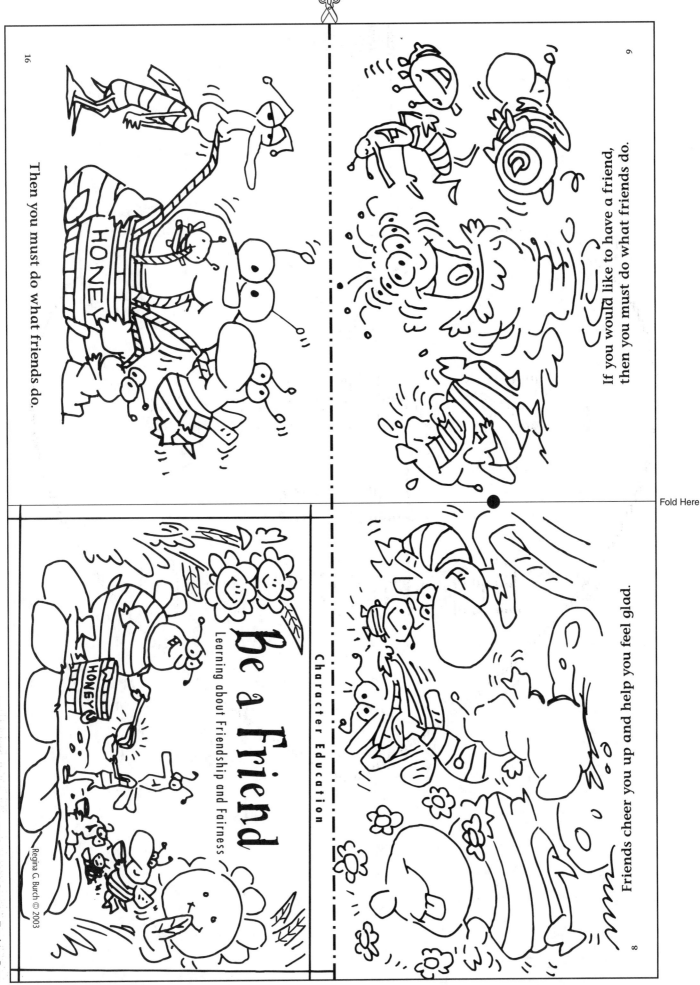

16

Then you must do what friends do.

9

If you would like to have a friend, then you must do what friends do.

Fold Here

●

Friends cheer you up and help you feel glad.

Character Education

Be a Friend

Learning about Friendship and Fairness

HONEY

8

When you are happy, when you feel great,

SPELLING BEE FINALS TODAY!

CAT

If you would like to have a friend,

HONEY

Fold Here

When you are lonely, when you are sad,

Friends, friends, you've got to have friends.

Character Education Resource Guide © 2003 Creative Teaching Press

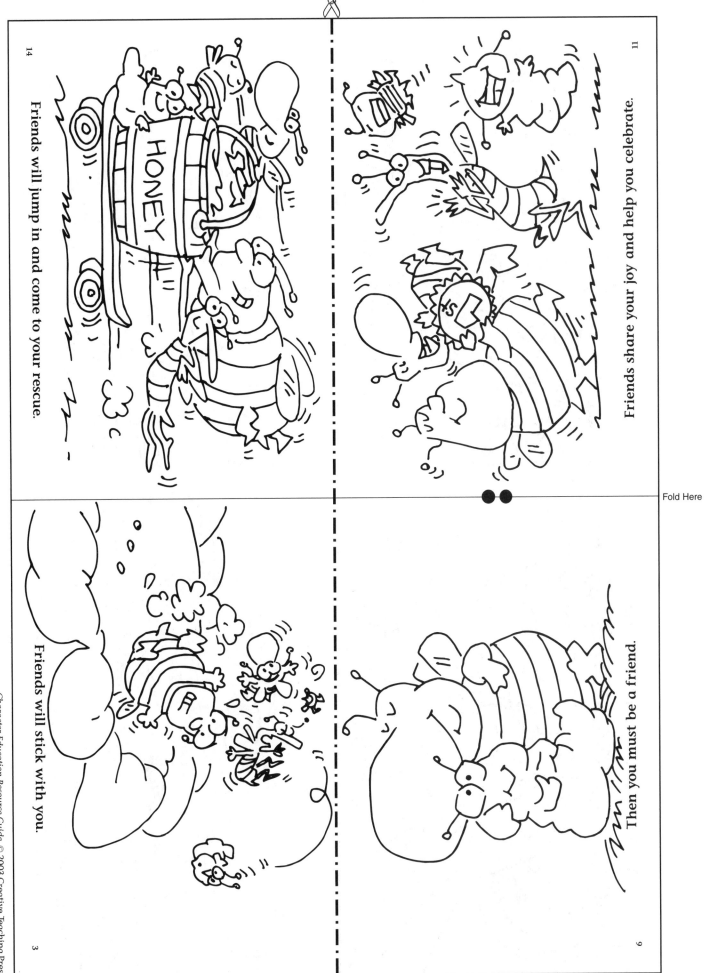

14

Friends will jump in and come to your rescue.

11

Friends share your joy and help you celebrate.

Fold Here

Friends will stick with you.

3

Then you must be a friend.

9

12

If you would like to have a friend,
then you must do what friends do.

13

When you have got a whole lot to do,

They'll be there till the end.

4

If you would like to have a friend,

5

Fold Here

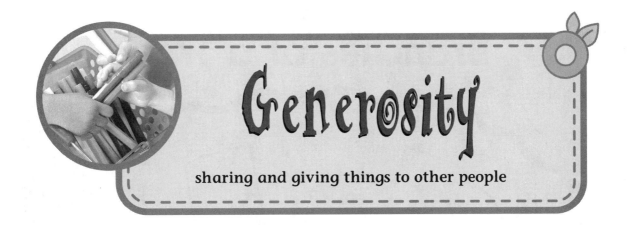

Generosity

sharing and giving things to other people

Generosity Trees

Copy the Branches of a Tree reproducible on an overhead transparency. Read aloud *The Giving Tree*. Display the transparency. Discuss with the class what generous acts the tree performed. Record each act on a separate branch of the tree. Give each child a Branches of a Tree reproducible. Ask children to try to perform several generous acts throughout the week or month. Each time children are generous, have them write about it on a branch of their tree. Invite children to share with the class all of the generous acts they performed. Cut out children's trees. Trace the tree shape on a piece of construction paper, and cut it out to make a book cover. Bind together children's trees to make a class book titled *Branches of Generosity*. Invite children to read the class book independently.

Materials
- ❤ *The Giving Tree* by Shel Silverstein
- ❤ Branches of a Tree reproducible (page 40)
- ❤ overhead projector/ transparency
- ❤ scissors
- ❤ construction paper
- ❤ bookbinding materials

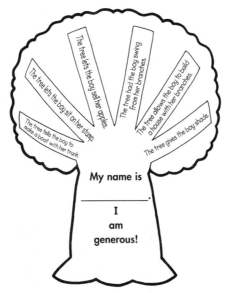

Pennies from Heaven

Read aloud *A Chair for My Mother*. Discuss the significance of helping another person and the sense of accomplishment the giver feels when he or she is generous. Help the class choose a charity (e.g., the Red Cross, a homeless shelter, a nonprofit group) to collect money for. Label a large jar *Pennies from Heaven,* and place it in the classroom. Ask children to place pennies in the jar for three or four months. Invite the class to help you count the pennies after all of the money is collected. Then, invite a representative from the chosen organization to come in and receive the gift.

Materials
- ❤ *A Chair for My Mother* by Vera B. Williams
- ❤ large jar
- ❤ label
- ❤ pennies (supplied by children)

Branches of a Tree

My name is

_____.

I
am
generous!

Character Education Resource Guide © 2003 Creative Teaching Press

16

9

Be generous with the things you own.

Sharing is caring. Be generous every day.
Sharing is caring. Be generous every day.

Fold Here

Sharing Is Caring

Learning about Generosity

Character Education

Sharing is caring. Be generous every day.
Sharing is caring. Be generous every day.

Regina G. Burch © 2003

8

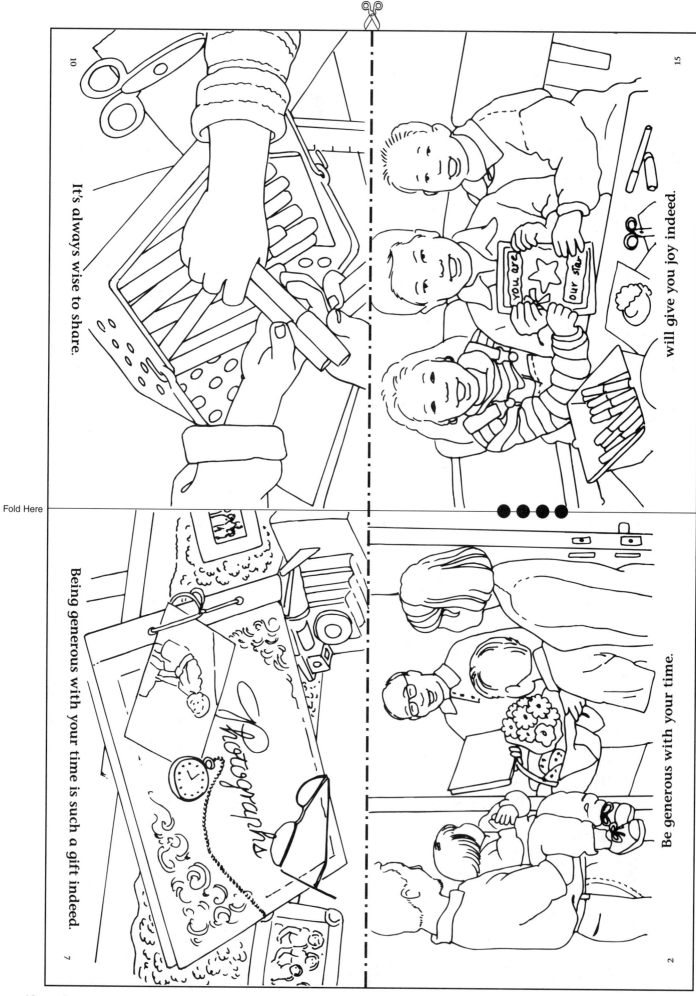

It's always wise to share.

10

will give you joy indeed.

15

Being generous with your time is such a gift indeed.

7

Be generous with your time.

2

Fold Here

Character Education Resource Guide © 2003 Creative Teaching Press

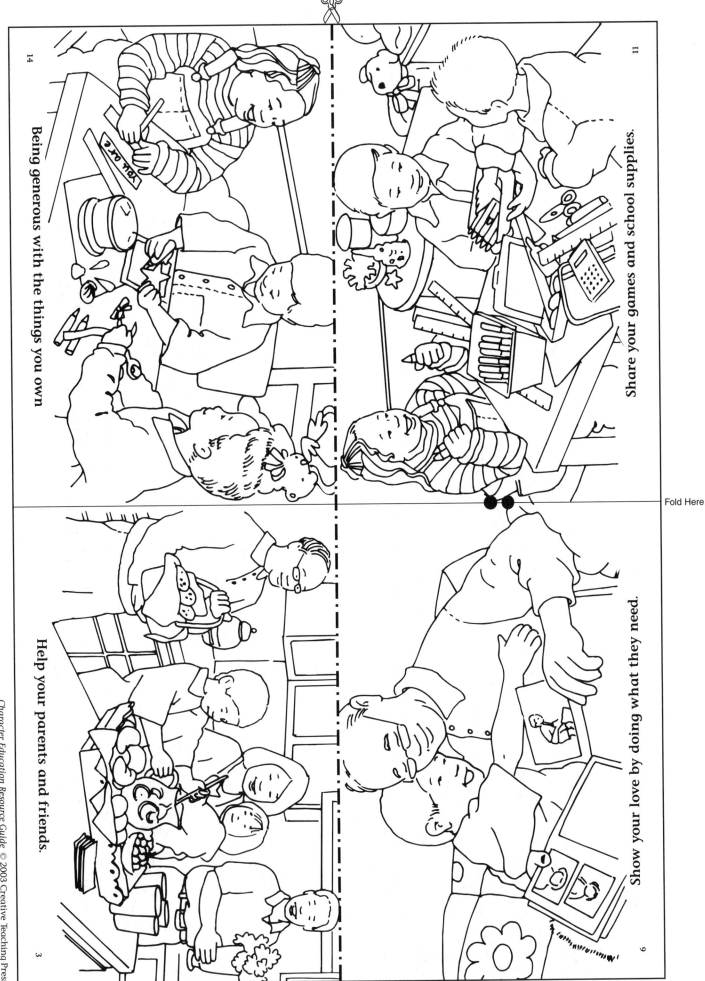

Share your games and school supplies.

Being generous with the things you own

Help your parents and friends.

Show your love by doing what they need.

Fold Here

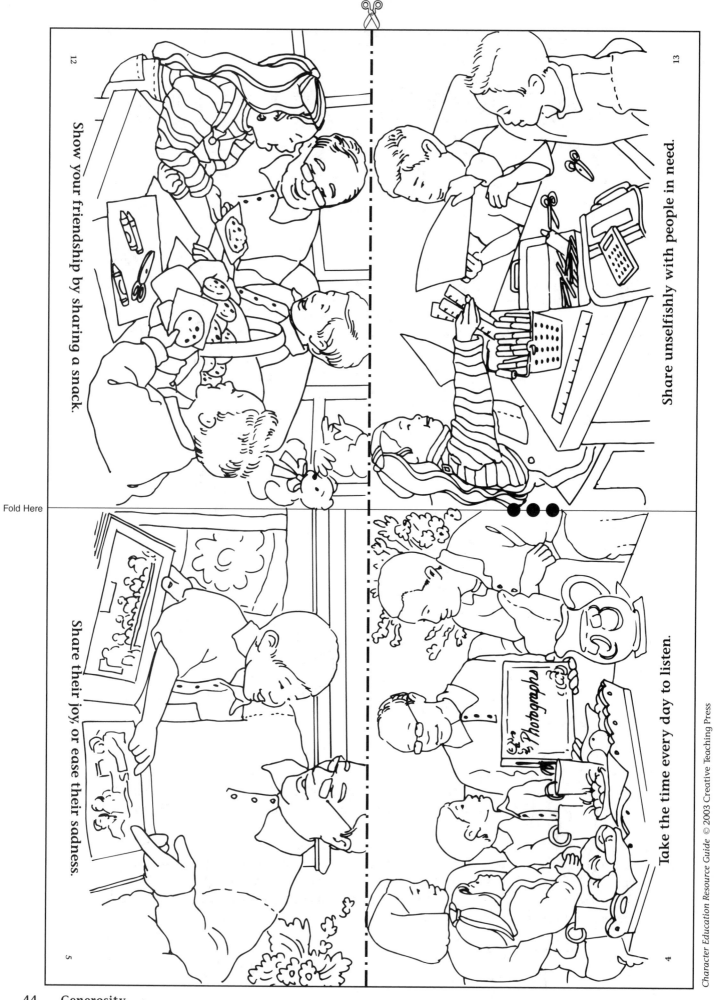

Show your friendship by sharing a snack.

Share unselfishly with people in need.

Share their joy, or ease their sadness.

Take the time every day to listen.

Character Education Resource Guide © 2003 Creative Teaching Press

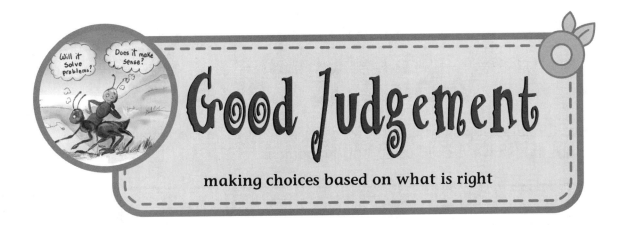

Good Judgement

making choices based on what is right

Make a Choice

Discuss with the class what good judgement is. Share a few examples. For example, say *Your mom tells you to get a snack from the kitchen. What do you choose?* Have children say what someone with good judgement would do and what someone with bad judgement would do. Give each child a Which Is Correct? reproducible. Read aloud the description of the scenario above each set of boxes. Ask children to describe what is happening in each picture. Then, have children circle the picture that shows the child who is using good judgement and draw an X over the picture that shows the child who is using bad judgement.

Materials
❤ Which Is Correct? reproducible (page 46)

Positive Statements

Discuss with the class what it means to use good judgement and to make good choices. Give examples of good choices (e.g., I think about what will happen before I do things, I share my snack with my friends when they don't have one). Ask the children to stand or sit in a circle. Hold a foam ball in your hands, and say something you do that shows you use good judgement. Then, toss or roll the ball to a child, and invite him or her to say a positive statement. Have children continue tossing the ball and saying positive statements until each child has had a turn.

Materials
❤ foam ball

Which Is Correct?

Directions: Circle each picture that shows a child using good judgement. Draw an X over each picture that shows a child using bad judgement.

Character Education Resource Guide © 2003 Creative Teaching Press

before you act!

Will it be fair?

Fold Here

Character Education

Would It be Right?

Learning about Good Judgement

Regina G. Burch © 2003

Will it be safe?

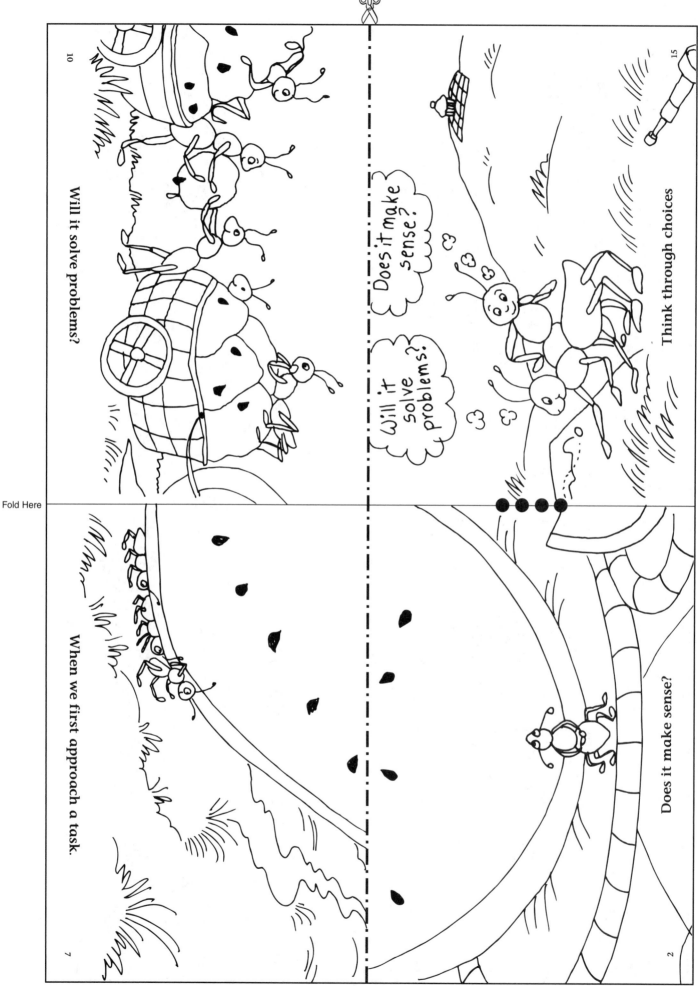

Will it solve problems?

Does it make sense?

Will it solve problems?

Think through choices

When we first approach a task.

Does it make sense?

Character Education Resource Guide © 2003 Creative Teaching Press

Does it show you care?

Will it be Safe?

Will it be fair?

So wait till you get all the facts.

Fold Here

These are the things we all must ask

Would it be right?

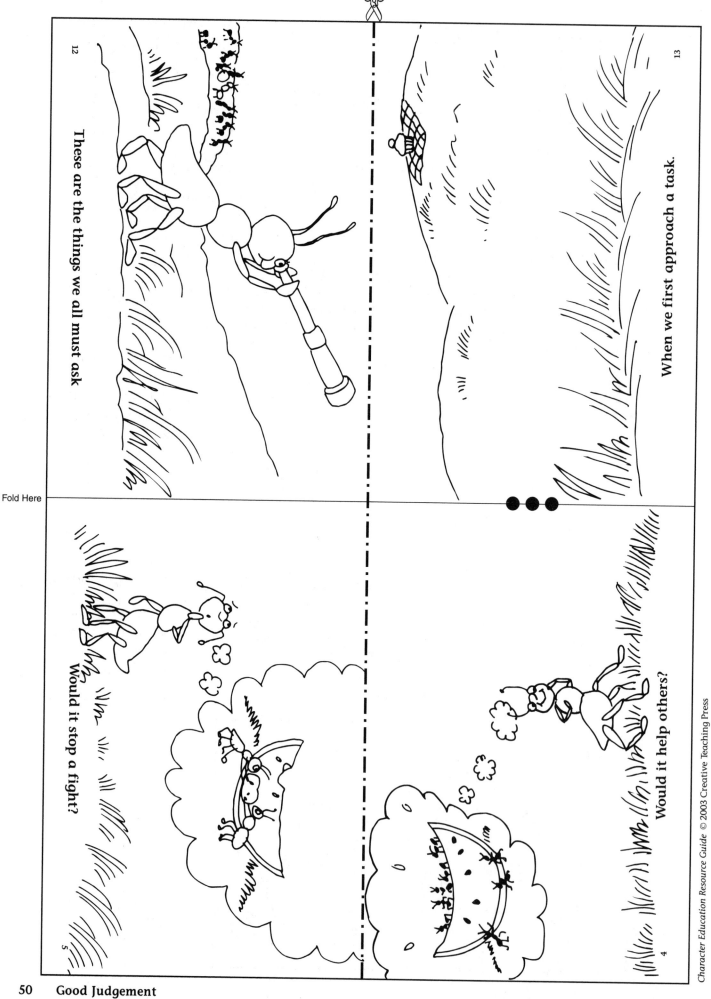

These are the things we all must ask

When we first approach a task.

Would it stop a fight?

Would it help others?

Character Education Resource Guide © 2003 Creative Teaching Press

Fold Here

Honesty

being sincere, truthful, trustworthy, and loyal

Honest Tees

Discuss honesty with the class. Ask children to explain what honesty is and describe ways people demonstrate that they are honest. Ask children to think of a time that they were honest. In advance, make several copies of the T-Shirt reproducible on tagboard, and cut them out to make patterns for children to trace. Have children trace a T-shirt on their favorite color of construction paper. Have children write about a time they demonstrated honesty and illustrate their writing. Then, ask children to cut out their shirt. Invite them to make a construction paper person and staple or glue their t-shirt on its body. Tell children to draw a face and add yarn or felt hair. Or, make a paper boy and a paper girl, and make two class books by stapling children's t-shirts on the bodies. Staple a T-Shirt reproducible over children's t-shirts to make book covers. Display the completed work, and encourage children to read each other's t-shirts.

Materials
- ❤ T-Shirt reproducible (page 52)
- ❤ tagboard
- ❤ scissors
- ❤ construction paper (assorted colors)
- ❤ crayons or markers
- ❤ glue (optional)
- ❤ yarn or felt

What Does a Lie Look Like?

Read aloud *A Big Fat Enormous Lie*. Discuss the lie from which the boy could not hide and how he made the monster go away. Ask children to describe what a lie, if alive, might look like. Have each child fold a sheet of construction paper in half and draw a vertical line down the center of the paper. Invite children to paint their interpretation of a living lie on one half of the paper and their interpretation of honesty on the other half. Encourage children to write a description under each painting. Display the paintings on a bulletin board titled *What You See Is What You Get!*

Materials
- ❤ *A Big Fat Enormous Lie* by Marjorie Weinman Sharmat
- ❤ construction paper
- ❤ watercolor paints
- ❤ paintbrushes

T-Shirt

Never Be Afraid
to Tell the Truth!

Everyone

Makes

Mistakes . . .

Character Education Resource Guide © 2003 Creative Teaching Press

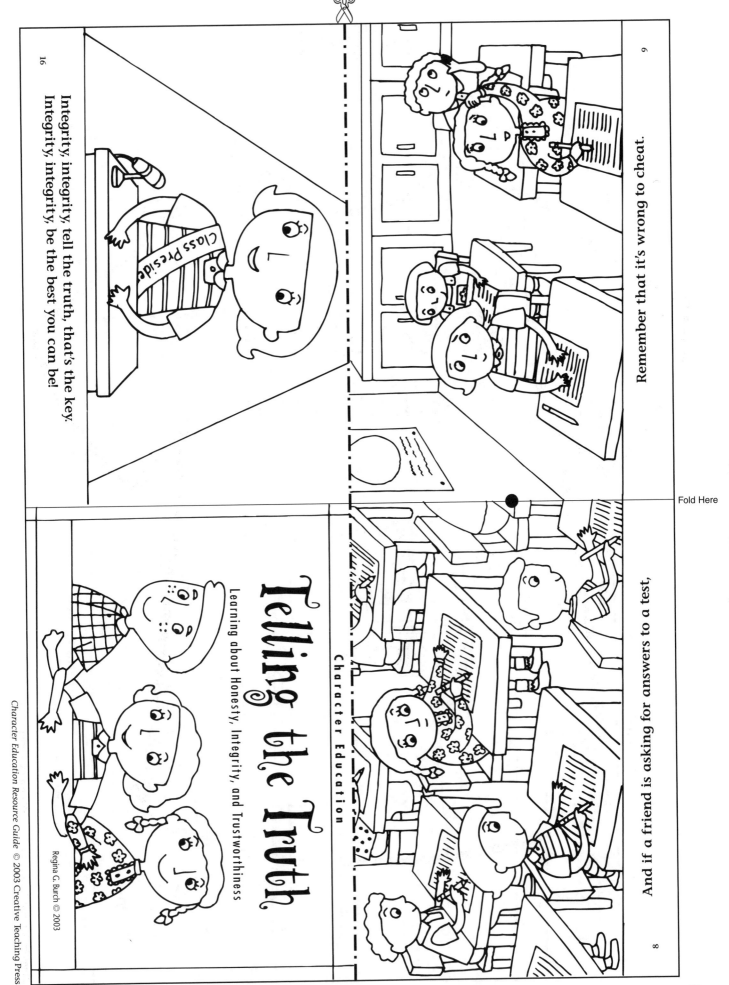

16

Integrity, integrity, tell the truth, that's the key.
Integrity, integrity, be the best you can be!

9

Remember that it's wrong to cheat.

Fold Here

Character Education

Telling the Truth

Learning about Honesty, Integrity, and Trustworthiness

Regina G. Burch © 2003

8

And if a friend is asking for answers to a test,

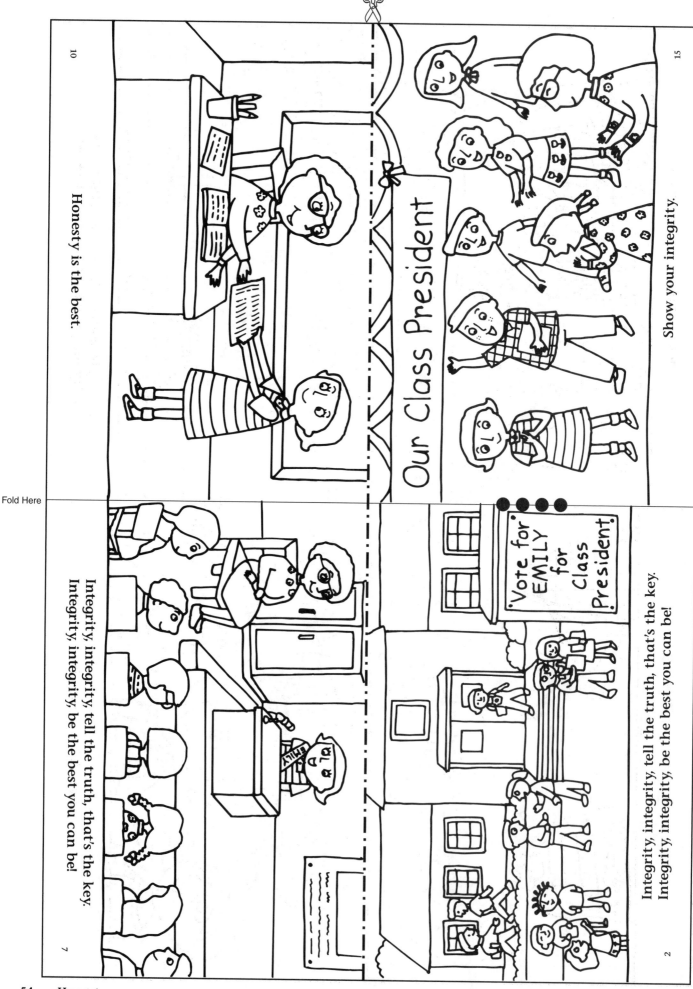

10

Honesty is the best.

Our Class President

15

Show your integrity.

Fold Here

Integrity, integrity, tell the truth, that's the key.
Integrity, integrity, be the best you can be!

7

Vote for EMILY for Class President.

Integrity, integrity, tell the truth, that's the key.
Integrity, integrity, be the best you can be!

2

Character Education Resource Guide © 2003 Creative Teaching Press

14

Someone else depends on you.

11

Integrity, integrity, tell the truth, that's the key.
Integrity, integrity, be the best you can be!

Congratulations EMILY

Fold Here

When someone asks a question,

Can you give us an extra recess?

and you'll have integrity.

3

9

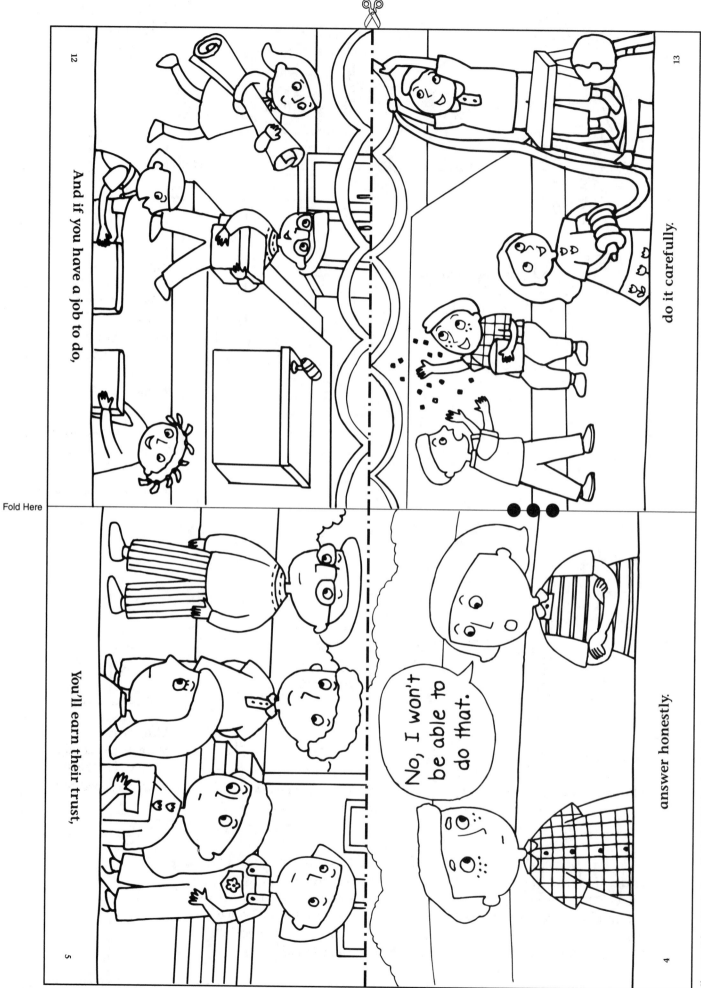

And if you have a job to do,

12

do it carefully.

13

You'll earn their trust,

5

answer honestly.

4

No, I won't be able to do that.

Character Education Resource Guide © 2003 Creative Teaching Press

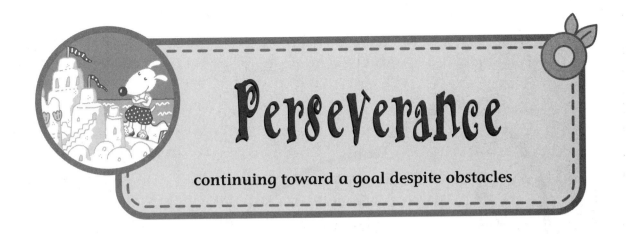

Perseverance

continuing toward a goal despite obstacles

Try, Try, Try . . .

Make several copies of the Flying Bird reproducible on tagboard, and cut them out to make patterns for children to trace. Write on the board *Try, try, try . . . and soon you'll fly!* Ask the class what they think this statement means. Discuss perseverance and the importance of trying no matter what the situation is. Read aloud *Three Cheers for Tacky*. Ask the class if Tacky showed perseverance, and invite children to share examples of what he did. Invite children to close their eyes and think of a time when they felt like Tacky. Ask volunteers to share their experiences. Have each child trace a bird pattern on a piece of construction paper and cut it out. Tell children to write about or draw a picture of a time they tried really hard to do something and finally accomplished it. Display children's birds on a bulletin board. Place the patterns you made from the reproducible along the top of the display.

Materials
- *Three Cheers for Tacky* by Helen Lester
- Flying Bird reproducible (page 58)
- tagboard
- scissors
- construction paper
- crayons or markers (optional)

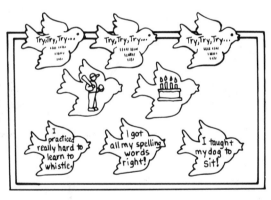

On the Slide

Place treats in a gift-wrapped box. Take the box outside, and place it on top of the slide (or another high location). Tell the class there are treats for them in the box if they can get it down. Explain the rules for retrieving the box: *No one's feet may leave the ground. No person may touch the box until it reaches the ground. Any item or combination of items in the classroom may be used to retrieve the box, but they may not be thrown or broken.* Invite children to brainstorm ways to retrieve the box. Invite them to make attempts until they successfully bring the box down. Pass out the treats. Discuss how the activity relates to the concept of perseverance. Ask questions such as *Was it easier or harder to persevere when you knew there would be a reward at the end? Why? What are some other activities you participate in that require perseverance? What kinds of rewards does perseverance in those activities bring?*

Materials
- treats (e.g., candy, pencils, stickers)
- gift-wrapped box

Flying Bird

Try, Try, Try . . .
And Soon
You'll
Fly!

Never give up.

But be patient and don't stop.

Fold Here

Your first try may be a flop,

Character Education

Never Give Up

Learning about Perseverance

Regina G. Burch © 2003

10

Never give up. Never give up.

15

Got to stick to it, got to keep trying.

Fold Here

Got to stick to it, got to keep trying. Never give up.

7

Never give up. Never give up.

2

11

14

Never give up. Never give up.

Got to stick to it, got to keep trying. Never give up.

Never give up. Never give up.

Got to stick to it, got to keep trying. Never give up.

Fold Here

3

6

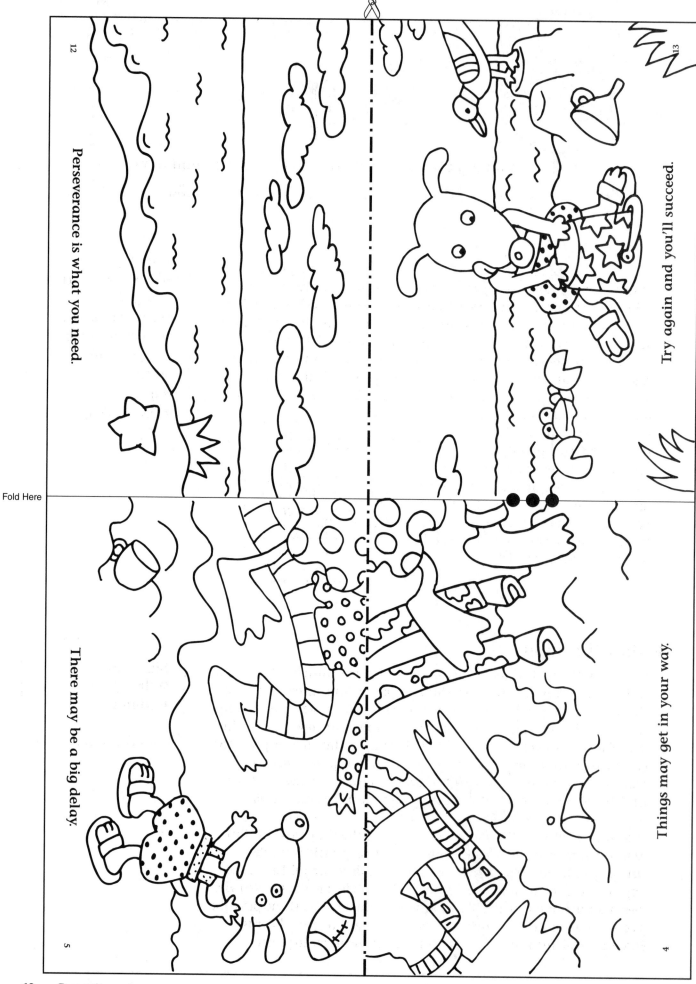

Perseverance is what you need.

12

Try again and you'll succeed.

13

There may be a big delay.

5

Things may get in your way.

4

Character Education Resource Guide © 2003 Creative Teaching Press

Fold Here

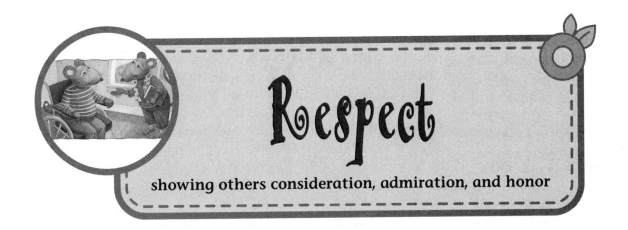

Respect

showing others consideration, admiration, and honor

Pockets Full of Respect

Copy a class set of the Pocket reproducible on colored construction paper. Discuss with the class the concept of respect. Ask children what types of things they should show respect for (e.g., people, places, things, nature). Give each child a pocket and several paper strips. Invite children to complete the sentence frame on their pocket by writing their name and the name of someone or something they have respect for. Then, have them write on separate paper strips how they show their respect. For example, if a child writes *Sam respects the forest!*, he or she can write *I don't throw trash on the ground* and *I leave animals alone.* Ask children to cut out their pocket and glue the edges (but not the top edge) of it to a sheet of construction paper. Tell them to slide their paper strips into their pocket so that they are sticking out at the top of it. Collect the pockets, and bind them into a class book titled *Pockets Full of Respect.* Invite children to read the book independently.

Materials
- ❤ Pocket reproducible (page 64)
- ❤ construction paper
- ❤ 8" (20 cm) white paper strips
- ❤ scissors
- ❤ glue
- ❤ bookbinding materials

Follow the Rules

Explain to children that following rules and being fair when playing a game with friends shows that they respect the people they are playing with. Ask children to name games they play in the classroom or outside at school (e.g., checkers, hide-and-seek). Record their responses on chart paper. Ask children to explain the rules of each game. Record the rules on the chart paper below or next to the corresponding game. Ask children to help you make a list of things they like to hear others say to them when playing games (e.g., *Good job, I like the way you did that, Can I please have the ball?*). Record their responses on another piece of chart paper. Invite children to play games and practice following the rules and saying respectful things to each other. Afterwards, ask children to make a list of things people said while they were playing (or in the past) that were hurtful or disrespectful. Record their responses on another piece of chart paper. (Ask children not to say who said these hurtful words.) Invite children to help you cut up this list and place the pieces in the trashcan, and remind them not to use disrespectful words. Encourage children to always make positive statements during games.

Materials
- ❤ chart paper
- ❤ scissors

Pocket

RESPECT

_____ respects

_____!

16

I know rules are good for me. I can show respect.

9

And I never call people names.

Fold Here

Character Education

Following the Rules

Learning about Respect

I'm fair to others when I play games.

8

10

I know rules are good for me. I can show respect.

15

I'm careful about the things I say.

Fold Here

7

I can show respect.

2

I know rules are good for me.

Character Education Resource Guide © 2003 Creative Teaching Press

I mind my teachers and my parents every day.

I always wait my turn in line.

Fold Here

Character Education Resource Guide © 2003 Creative Teaching Press

I can show respect.

I know rules are good for me.

I obey the rules and all the signs.

Wash Hands

DON'T WALK

Quiet

DO NOT RUN

I know rules are good for me. I can show respect.

Fold Here

I take good care of property.

I look at others when they talk to me.

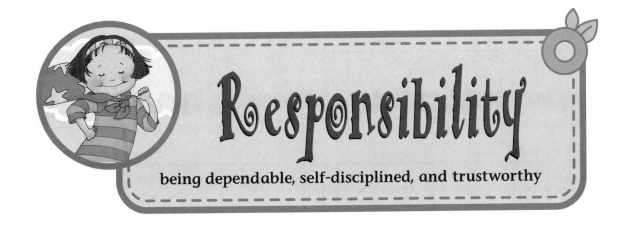

Responsibility

being dependable, self-disciplined, and trustworthy

Reward Responsibility

Copy a class set of the Responsibility Chart. Discuss with the class what it means to be responsible. Ask children what type of responsibilities they have at school (e.g., concentrate, turn in homework, raise your hand). Meet with each child individually. Ask each child what responsibilities he or she wants to focus on improving. (You can use the chart to have children focus on one, two, or three responsibilities.) Record children's responses on their chart. Then, ask children what reward they would like for being responsible (e.g., extra reading time, play a game on the computer, lunch with the teacher). Decide how many times (depending on what responsibility he or she is focusing on) the child should have to demonstrate his or her responsibility before being rewarded. Staple each child's chart inside a separate manila folder. Praise children and put a sticker in the appropriate column on their chart each time they achieve their task. Make sure children understand that their behavior or actions made a difference. For example, say *When Sam raised his hand, he didn't interrupt Susie when she was speaking.* Give children rewards when they have proven they can be responsible. To extend the activity, send home the charts and encourage children to be more responsible at home.

Cut and Collage

Divide the class into small groups. Give each group several magazines. Ask children to locate and cut out pictures that show people being responsible (e.g., brushing their teeth, wearing a seat belt, walking across a street in a crosswalk when the light is green). Give each group a butcher paper square, and ask children to glue their pictures on their paper to make a collage. Explain that a collage can have pictures overlapping each other. Invite groups to share their collage with the class. Have children explain how each picture on their collage illustrates responsibility. Bind together the collages to make a class book, and place it in the classroom library so children can look at it.

Name _____ Month _____

Responsibility Chart

Responsibility #1	Responsibility #2	Responsibility #3
_____	_____	_____
_____	_____	_____
_____	_____	_____
Reward #1	Reward #2	Reward #3
_____	_____	_____

Character Education Resource Guide © 2003 Creative Teaching Press

You can count on me.

I keep my promises to my friends.

Fold Here

You Can Count on Me

Learning about Responsibility

Character Education

Regina G. Burch © 2003

You can count on me.

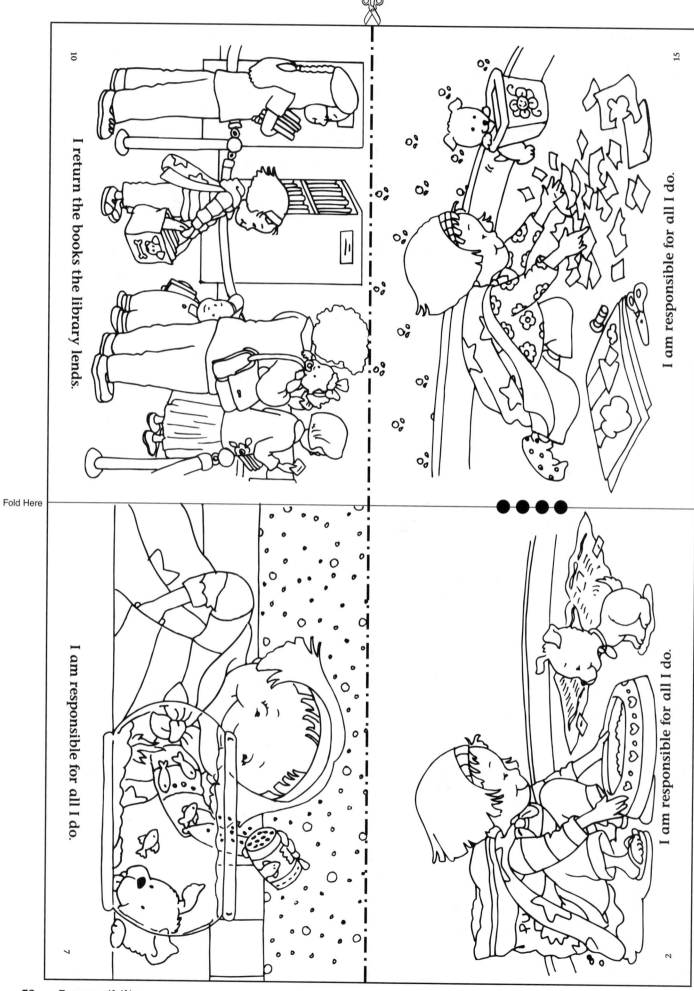

I return the books the library lends.

10

I am responsible for all I do.

15

I am responsible for all I do.

7

I am responsible for all I do.

2

Character Education Resource Guide © 2003 Creative Teaching Press

Fold Here

I keep up with the things I own.

I am responsible for all I do.

Fold Here

You can count on me.

I try to practice the golden rule.

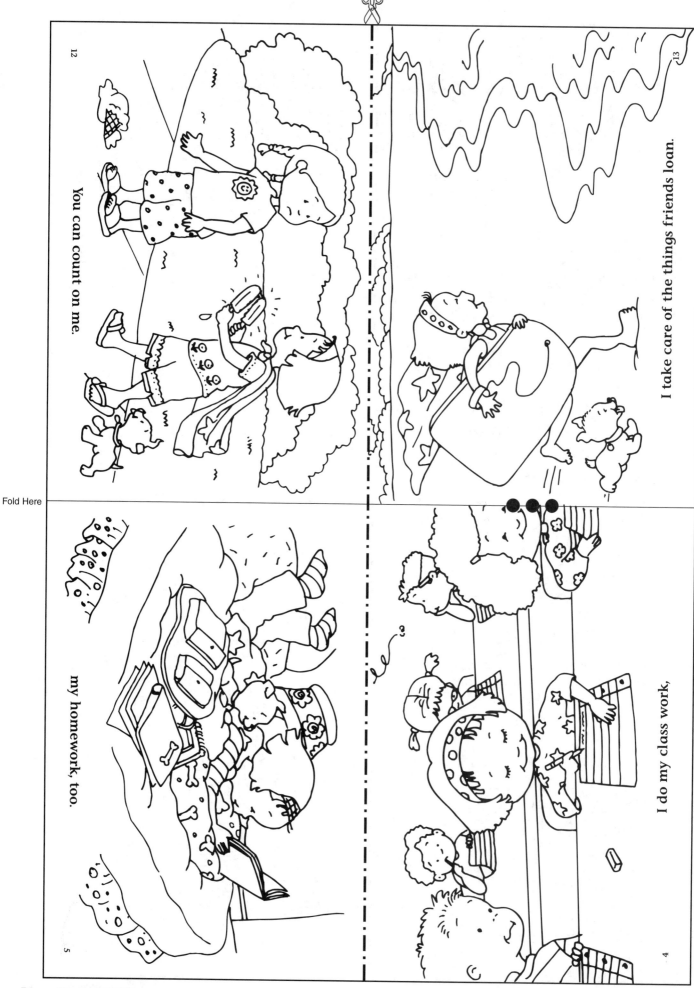

You can count on me.

my homework, too.

I take care of the things friends loan.

I do my class work,

Character Education Resource Guide © 2003 Creative Teaching Press

Fold Here

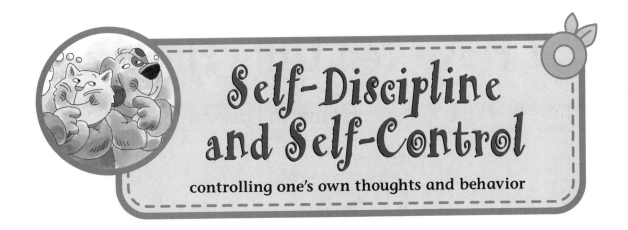

Self-Discipline and Self-Control

controlling one's own thoughts and behavior

I Have Ten Little Fingers

Copy a class set of the poem "I Have Ten Little Fingers." Make an enlarged copy of the poem by writing it on chart paper or copying the reproducible onto an overhead transparency. Give each child a copy of the poem, and display the enlarged copy. Teach the poem and the fingerplay to the class to help children focus their attention, get ready to listen, and set the stage for self-discipline.

Materials
❤ "I Have Ten Little Fingers" poem (page 76)
❤ chart paper or overhead projector/ transparency

Toss a Rule

Write a sentence about self-discipline or self-control (e.g., *I think before I do things, I keep my hands to myself, I choose healthy snacks*) on chart paper. Read aloud the sentence, and use a pointer to point to each word so all the children are familiar with the words in the sentence. Give a beanbag to a child. Ask him or her to say the first word in the sentence and then toss the beanbag to another child. Have the next child say the second word and toss the beanbag to someone else. Have children continue to read the rest of the sentence. Repeat this process with several sentences. This game reinforces positive behavior. It also helps children understand that each group of letters separated by white space is a word and reinforces one-to-one correspondence, which is an important print concept that is necessary as children learn to read. For more advanced children, have them say the word and how many syllables it has.

Materials
❤ chart paper
❤ pointer
❤ beanbag

I Have Ten Little Fingers

I have ten little fingers and they all belong to me.

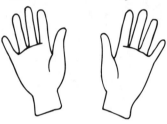

I can make them do things. Would you like to see?

I can shut them tight. I can open them wide.

I can put them together. I can make them hide.

I can make them wave high. I can make them wave low.

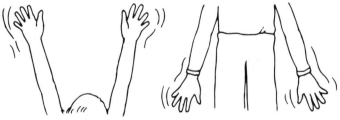

I can fold them quietly and hold them just so.

Character Education Resource Guide © 2003 Creative Teaching Press

Having self-control will help you meet your goals, oh, oh, oh.

Walk away from a fight, oh, oh, oh.

Fold Here

Think Before You Act

Learning about Self-Discipline and Self-Control

Character Education

¡NO!

Just say "no."

10

Every day, you need self-control.

15

Every day, you need self-control.

Keep your hands to yourself.

7

Think before you act.

2

14

Spend your money wisely, oh, oh, oh.

11

Having self-control will help you meet your goals, oh, oh, oh.

3

Eat healthy foods so you'll grow.

9

Having self-control will help you meet your goals, oh, oh, oh.

Fold Here

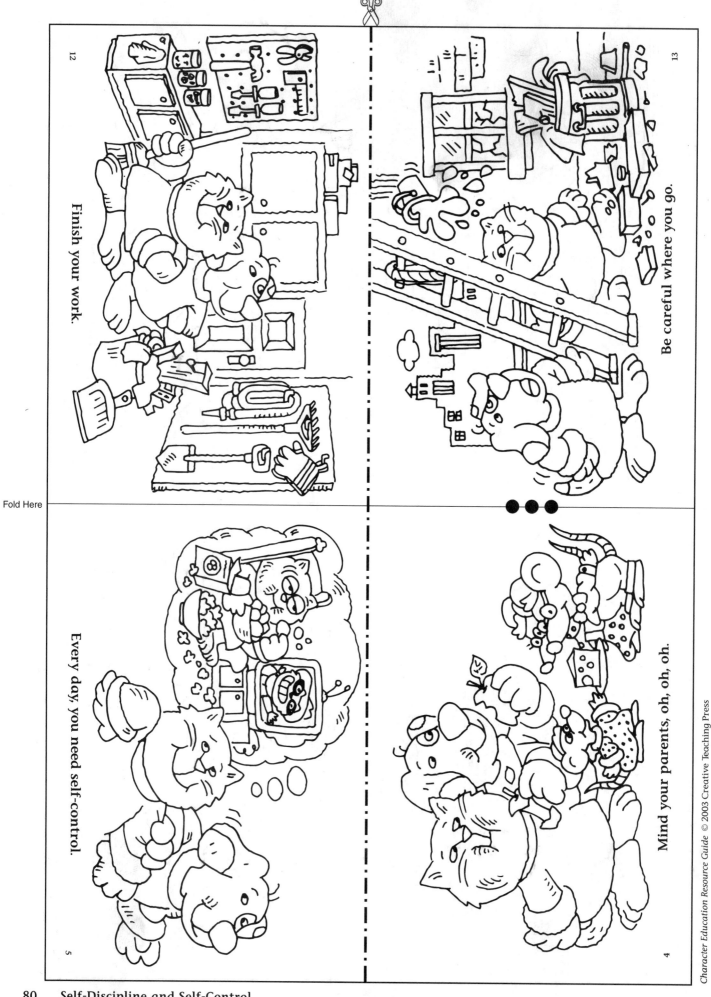

Finish your work.

Be careful where you go.

Fold Here

Every day, you need self-control.

Mind your parents, oh, oh, oh.

Character Education Resource Guide © 2003 Creative Teaching Press